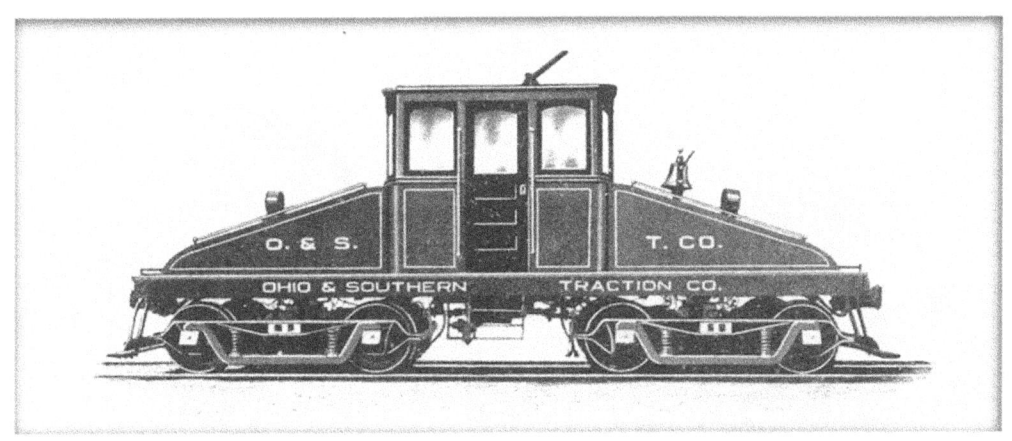

Trolley Cars and Locomotives of the McGuire-Cummings Manufacturing Company

©2010 PERISCOPE FILM LLC
ALL RIGHTS RESERVED
ISBN #978-1-935700-33-3
WWW.PERISCOPEFILM.COM

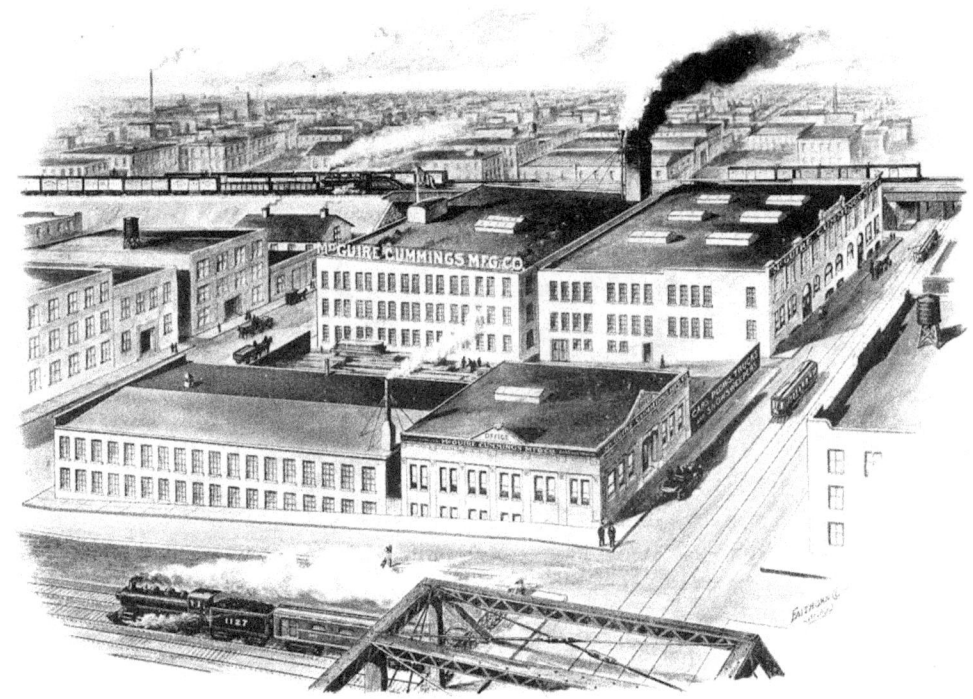

GENERAL OFFICES AND PLANT AT CHICAGO

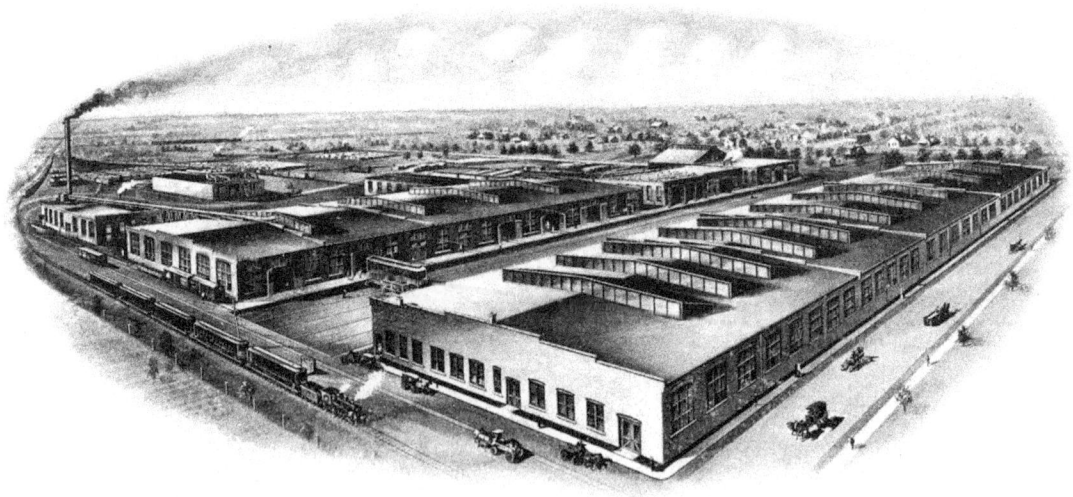

PARIS (ILL.) PLANT OF McGUIRE-CUMMINGS MANUFACTURING COMPANY

This is one of the largest and best equipped car building plants in the United States. It covers 30 acres, and is located on the Big Four-New York Central Lines, Cairo Division Big Four, the Vandalia-Pennsylvania System and also has connections with the Terre Haute, Indianapolis & Eastern Railway (electric).

INTERURBAN CARS

REPRESENTATIVE types of modern interurban cars are illustrated in the pages immediately following. With a few exceptions, these cars have composite underframes which are favored by operating managers of many of the leading electric roads in the country. This is due largely to the fact that it is now possible to design and build underframes of semi-steel or all-steel construction without materially increasing the weight over those built of wood. For interurban travel, which frequently traverses miles of uneven country at high speed, cars with strong underframes are vitally necessary, and yet, minimum weight is an equally important factor.

The underframe combining both maximum strength and minimum weight is the underframe most desired. This combination depends to a large degree upon the excellence of the engineering design and that essential is the product only of the highest engineering ability and the most expert mechanical skill.

Special training and years of experience have qualified our engineers and craftsmen in all phases of car construction, with the result that in placing your orders for cars with this company, you are assured at the outset that the engineering designs—the fundamentals of your cars—are sound in principle and correct in execution.

Equal attention is given to the equipment, the superstructure and the interior arrangement so as to insure maximum efficiency and durability in service and a minimum expense for maintenance.

Our engineers are at all times at the disposal of our patrons, in submitting specifications, blue-prints and full information.

INTERURBAN

Combination Passenger and Baggage Car

For single end operation. Underframe of steel construction, a feature of which is a deafening floor, packed with mineral wool to deaden vibration and noise. Interior finish mahogany; ceiling semi-Empire type. Seating capacity, including smoking compartment, 60 passengers. Car is provided with saloon and hot water heater. M. C. B. radial couplers. Mounted on McGuire-Cummings No. 70-A, M. C. B. high speed trucks.

GENERAL DIMENSIONS

Length over buffers	56 feet 0 inches
Length over vestibules	55 feet 0 inches
Length from body corner post to baggage door post	44 feet 11 inches
Width over all	9 feet 6 inches
Width over side sills	9 feet 2¼ inches
Width inside	8 feet 5¼ inches
Distance between deck sills	5 feet 2 inches
Height top of rail to top of trolley board	13 feet 6¾ inches
Height top of rail to bottom of sill	3 feet 5 inches
Height bottom of sill to top of running board	10 feet 1¾ inches
Height top of floor to top of window capping	2 feet 4 inches
Height top of sill to bottom of side plate	6 feet 8⅜ inches
Height top of floor to finish under deck sill	7 feet 4¼ inches
Truck centers	35 feet 6 inches
Wheel base	6 feet 6 inches

INTERURBAN

For Long Haul Interurban Service

Combination passenger and baggage car for single end operation. Extra roomy, flush platform. Folding doors, acting as partition, afford wide opening for ingress and egress of passengers. Underframe of composite type. Interior finish golden oak. Seating capacity 60 passengers. Hot water heaters. Standard M. C. B. couplers and draft gear. McGuire-Cummings No. 70-A, M. C. B. high speed trucks.

GENERAL DIMENSIONS

Length over buffers	57 feet 6¾ inches
Length over body corner posts	48 feet 3¾ inches
Width over all	9 feet 2½ inches
Width over side sills	8 feet 10⅜ inches
Width inside between posts	8 feet 2⅞ inches
Width inside below arm rail	8 feet 1¾ inches
Width between deck sills	4 feet 10 inches
Height top of rail to underside of sill (car body light)	3 feet 0 inches
Height from under side of sill to top of roof	9 feet 8 inches
Height from top of rail to top of roof	12 feet 8 inches
Height top of sill to bottom of plate	6 feet 7¼ inches
Height from floor to window rest	2 feet 5 inches
Height from top of rail to center of draw bar	2 feet 10½ inches
Height from rail to top of trolley board	12 feet 10½ inches
Truck centers	35 feet 3¾ inches
Wheel base	6 feet 6 inches

INTERURBAN

Combination Express and Passenger Car

This is a single end combination express and passenger car. Underframe is of the composite type. Interior finish golden oak. Ceiling and headlining, bird's-eye maple. Seating capacity 54 passengers. Equipped with Standard M. C. B. couplers and draft gear. Mounted on McGuire-Cummings No. 20-A, M. C. B. trucks.

GENERAL DIMENSIONS

Length over all	51 feet 7 inches
Length over vestibules	50 feet 7 inches
Width over posts	8 feet 10¾ inches
Width over all	9 feet 2 inches
Height from top of rail to top of trolley board	12 feet 11 inches
Height from top of rail to underside of sill	3 feet 5 inches
Height from bottom of sill to top of running board	9 feet 6 inches
Height from top of floor to window capping	2 feet 4 inches
Truck centers	31 feet 6 inches
Wheel base	6 feet 3 inches

INTERURBAN

Combination Passenger and Baggage Car

Designed for double end operation. Composite underframe. Interior of oak, dark Flemish finish. Prismatic Gothics. Seating capacity in main compartment, 48 passengers. In baggage room, which can be used as smoker, there are seats for 10. Car is provided with hot water heater. Equipped with M. C. B. radial couplers and mounted on McGuire-Cummings No. 10-A, M. C. B. trucks.

GENERAL DIMENSIONS

Length over buffers	52 feet 6 inches
Length of baggage compartment	10 feet 2 inches
Length of passenger compartment	31 feet 3 inches
Width over sills	8 feet 8 inches
Width over all	9 feet 0 inches
Width between posts	8 feet 1 inch
Height from rails to top of roof	12 feet 10 inches
Height from rails to under side of sill	3 feet 4 inches
Height from top of rail to center of coupler	2 feet 10½ inches
Truck centers	31 feet 0 inches
Wheel base	6 feet 0 inches

INTERURBAN

Private, Business and Inspection Car

Elaborately designed and equipped throughout for comfort, convenience and the full transaction of business en route. Has office, dining and smoking rooms with sofa beds. Also kitchen, buffet, saloon and observation parlor. Underframe composite type. Interior African mahogany with carvings and tulip, ebony and satinwood inlays. Hot water heater and forced draft ventilators. Equipped with M. C. B. radial couplers. Mounted on McGuire-Cummings No. 70-A, M. C. B. high speed trucks.

GENERAL DIMENSIONS

Length over buffers	51 feet 0 inches
Length over vestibules	49 feet 8 inches
Width over posts	8 feet 7½ inches
Width over all	8 feet 10 inches
Distance between deck sills	5 feet 2 inches
Height from top of rail to top of trolley board	12 feet 4 inches
Height from top of rail to bottom of sill	3 feet 2 inches
Height from bottom of sill to top of running board	9 feet 2 inches
Height from top of floor to top of window capping	2 feet 4 inches
Truck centers	27 feet 0 inches
Wheel base	6 feet 3 inches

INTERURBAN

Passenger, Express and Milk Car

This car, which has extra heavy trussing, is specially designed for the handling of milk on the early morning runs. The underframe is of the composite type, heavily reinforced. Seating capacity 54 passengers. Interior is of white ash, natural finish. Ceiling is of 3-ply veneer. Baggage room of carline finish. Car has hot water heater, is equipped with McGuire-Cummings standard radial spring draw bar and is mounted on McGuire-Cummings No. 10-A, M. C. B. trucks.

GENERAL DIMENSIONS

Length of car body over buffers	41 feet 6¼ inches
Length of platform	5 feet 3⅜ inches
Length inside passenger compartment (center partition to end panel)	18 feet 6 inches
Length of baggage compartment (back of motorman's rail)	15 feet 6 inches
Length of door openings	4 feet 0 inches
Width of car over side sills	8 feet 4 inches
Total width of car at eaves	8 feet 8 inches
Truck centers	24 feet 0 inches
Wheel base	6 feet 0 inches

INTERURBAN

Adapted For Heavy Excursion Service

In use where the Saturday and Sunday and excursion business is very heavy. Divided into passenger and smoking compartments. Thirty-six passengers can be seated in main compartment and 16 in smoker. Underframe is of composite type and interior is finished in quarter-sawed oak. Ceilings are of bird's-eye maple. Car is provided with saloon. Mounted on McGuire-Cummings No. 10-A, M. C. B. trucks.

GENERAL DIMENSIONS

Length over all	47 feet 10 inches
Length over dash	46 feet 6 inches
Length over corner posts	36 feet 6 inches
Width over sills	8 feet 5 inches
Width over all	8 feet 9 inches
Height bottom of sill to top of roof	9 feet 5 inches
Truck centers	24 feet 0 inches
Wheel base	6 feet 6 inches

INTERURBAN

Smaller Type Car for Suburban Service

Car body is 29 feet in length, with drop platforms, and is designed for double end operation. In the main compartment there are seats for 32 passengers and in the baggage room, accommodations for 10. Interior is of oak. Underframe is of the composite type. Car is provided with electric heaters and mounted on McGuire-Cummings No. 39-A trucks.

GENERAL DIMENSIONS

Length of car body over buffers	40 feet 8 inches
Length of car body over vestibule	39 feet 6 inches
Length over corner posts	29 feet 2 inches
Length of platform at inside of vestibule baggage end	4 feet 6 inches
Length of platform at inside of vestibule passenger end	5 feet 0 inches
Width over window rail	8 feet 9 inches
Extreme width of car body	8 feet 11 inches
Height of car body (from under side of sill to top of trolley board)	9 feet 4 inches
Height from top of car platform floor to top of brake handle	3 feet 10 inches
Truck centers	18 feet 0 inches
Wheel base	4 feet 3 inches

INTERURBAN

Passenger, Baggage and Smoking Car

Extra roomy car for long, through "limited" service. Length over all is 58 feet 6 inches. For double-end operation. Seating capacity, 38 in main compartment, 16 in smoker, 10 in baggage room and collapsible chairs for 6 additional. Underframe of the composite type. Interior finish golden oak. Equipped with M. C. B. radial couplers and mounted on McGuire-Cummings No. 70-A, M. C. B. high speed trucks.

GENERAL DIMENSIONS

Length over buffers	58 feet 6 inches
Length over vestibules	57 feet 6 inches
Width over posts	8 feet 8 inches
Width over all	8 feet 11½ inches
Height from top of rail to top of trolley board	13 feet 0 inches
Height from top of rail to under side of sill	3 feet 5 inches
Height from bottom of sill to top of running board	9 feet 7 inches
Truck centers	33 feet 10 inches
Wheel base	6 feet 6 inches

INTERURBAN

For Hauling Trailers and Sleeping Cars

Combination express, mail and smoking car, designed for exceedingly heavy motor service. This car is giving excellent service in long "through" runs. Underframe of composite type. Interior finish mahogany in smoker and ash in other compartments, with carline finish. Has seats for 16 passengers. Provided with hot water heater and saloon. Equipped with M. C. B. radial couplers.

GENERAL DIMENSIONS

Length of car over all	52 feet 6 inches
Width of car over side sill	9 feet 1¼ inches
Width of car over sheathing	9 feet 3 inches
Width over all at eaves	9 feet 5⅜ inches
Width of car inside, between sheathing	8 feet 5 inches
Height from bottom of sill to top of roof boards	9 feet 4⅞ inches
Height between top of sill and bottom of side plates	7 feet ¼ inch
Height from top of rail to under side of sill	3 feet 5 inches
Height from rail to center of draw bar	2 feet 10 inches
Truck centers	35 feet 0 inches
Wheel base	6 feet 6 inches

INTERURBAN

Trailer for Heavy Excursion Service

This roomy car, which has a seating capacity for 48 passengers and can accommodate as many more standing, is especially adaptable as a trail car for heavy excursion service. Underframe is of composite type. Interior finish is golden oak. Has "Monitor" roof. Is equipped with electric heaters and mounted on McGuire-Cummings No. 10-A, M. C. B. trucks.

GENERAL DIMENSIONS

Length over all	44 feet 0 inches
Length over buffers	43 feet 0 inches
Width over panels	8 feet 7½ inches
Width over all	8 feet 11¼ inches
Height from top of rail to top of trolley board	12 feet 0 inches
Height from top of rail to under side of sill	2 feet 6 inches
Height from bottom of sill to top of running board	9 feet 0 inches
Truck centers	23 feet 0 inches
Wheel base	6 feet 0 inches

CITY CARS

OWING to the great diversity in designs of city cars, and the wide variance in operating conditions, the type of car best adapted for use in city service is practically dictated by local conditions. Although the wood underframe is largely in use and practical for ordinary city service, there is a tendency toward the built-up underframe for this type of car. The design of the superstructure depends entirely upon operating conditions and the class of service required. Extreme roominess, consistent with local service conditions, is always desired in the construction of city cars and this is a feature to which our engineers devote special attention.

In city service especially, the weight of the car is an important factor and one deserving of the most careful consideration. Quick starts and stops are essential to the maintenance of schedules in city service.

The bulky, unwieldly car means an excess of dead weight, slow acceleration in starting, and, owing to its great momentum, difficult stopping. On the other hand, with the heavy traffic to which city cars are subject during the "rush" hours, it is imprudent as well as extremely hazardous to construct other than the strongest and most substantial cars for this class of service.

Well built cars mean less maintenance expense and greater car mileage. It therefore is the aim of this company to turn out city cars which shall possess the requisite lightness in weight and at the same time prove thoroughly trustworthy as to strength and durability.

We shall be pleased to submit blue prints, specifications, and full information covering any phase of the subject, on request.

CITY CARS

Double Truck. Pay-As-You-Enter Type

For double-end operation. Thirty-foot body. All-steel underframe with seven-foot drop platforms. Roof of the Monitor type. Straight sides. Folding steps. Reversible seats, accommodating 40 passengers and standing room for as many more. Interior finish golden oak. Mounted on McGuire-Cummings No. 10-A. M. C. B. trucks.

GENERAL DIMENSIONS

Length over all	44 feet 0 inches
Length over vestibule	43 feet 0 inches
Length over car body end posts	30 feet 0 inches
Width over all	8 feet 4 inches
Width inside	7 feet 9 inches
Height from top of rail to underside of sill	2 feet 9 inches
Height from under side of sill to trolley board	8 feet 8½ inches
Height from top of rail to trolley board	11 feet 7½ inches
Truck centers	19 feet 0 inches
Wheel base	6 feet 0 inches

CITY CARS

For Ordinary Fare Collection

Single truck car for city service; double end operation, wood underframe, reinforced drop platform with folding gates. Body, 20 feet 8 inches with concave convex sides. Interior finish solid mahogany with embossed mouldings; ceiling of bird's-eye maple. Cross seats of the "Walk-over" type, accommodating 28 passengers. Equipped with special automatic ventilators. Mounted on McGuire-Cummings solid steel Columbian truck.

GENERAL DIMENSIONS

Length of car body over buffers..................30 feet 8 inches
Length over corner posts of car body..............20 feet 8 inches
Height of car body (from under side of sill to extreme top of roof)......9 feet ¾ inches
Extreme width of car body........................8 feet 2½ inches
Width of car body on sills over panels............7 feet 7½ inches
Wheel base......................................7 feet 6 inches

CITY CARS

"Pay-Within" Type, 21 Foot 8 Inch Body

Double end operation. Underframe of wood with reinforced drop platforms. Concave convex sides, "turtleback" roof. Interior finish cherry. Cross seats of the "Walk-over" type for 32 passengers. Provided with electric heaters. Mounted on McGuire-Cummings solid steel Columbian truck.

GENERAL DIMENSIONS

Length of car body over buffers..................33 feet 8 inches
Length of car body over corner posts..............21 feet 8 inches
Length of platform to outside of dash at center....5 feet 6 inches
Width of car body over window rails...............8 feet 0 inches
Height from top of rail to top of roof at center..10 feet 10½ inches
Height from top of rail to bottom of side sill....2 feet 5¾ inches
Wheel base......................................7 feet 6 inches

CITY CARS

Single Truck and Single End Operation

This car has 22-foot body, with straight sides. The underframe is of wood, with reinforced drop platform. Interior of golden oak, with composite board ceiling. Cross seats of the "Walk-over" type, affording accommodation for 32 passengers. Has electric heaters. Mounted on McGuire-Cummings solid steel Columbian truck.

GENERAL DIMENSIONS

Length of car body over buffers	32 feet 2 inches
Length of car body over end panel, at sill	22 feet 0 inches
Width of car at sill, including panels	8 feet 1½ inches
Width of car body over posts, above belt rail	8 feet 5¼ inches
Width over sheathing	8 feet 3¼ inches
Width inside	7 feet 6 inches
Height from top of rail to under side of sill	2 feet 6 inches
Height from underside of sill to top of roof	9 feet ¾ inches
Height from top of rail to top of roof	11 feet 6¾ inches
Wheel base	7 feet 0 inches

CITY CARS

Single Truck Pay-As-You-Enter Type

For double end operation. This car has a 20-foot 8-inch body, reinforced drop platform and concave convex sides. The underframe is of wood. Interior finish mahogany. Seats are of the "Walk-over" type, accommodating 32 passengers. Equipped with McGuire-Cummings radial drawbar and mounted on McGuire-Cummings solid steel Columbian truck.

GENERAL DIMENSIONS

Length over all	32 feet 8 inches
Length over vestibule	31 feet 8 inches
Width over posts above belt rail	8 feet 2 inches
Height from top of rail to under side of sill	2 feet 6 inches
Height from under side of sill to trolley board	9 feet 6 inches
Height from top of rail to trolley board	12 feet 0 inches
Wheel base	7 feet 6 inches

CITY CARS

Single Truck, Center Aisle, Open Car

Specially designed for the rapid handling of passengers during hours of heavy traffic. Light weight, but substantially built car for summer service. Seating capacity, 40 passengers. Has malleable iron concave convex panels. Underframe of wood. Interior finish ash. Equipped with radial coupler and mounted on McGuire-Cummings A-1 suspension truck.

GENERAL DIMENSIONS

Length over all .... 28 feet 9 inches
Length over vestibule .... 27 feet 9 inches
Width over all .... 7 feet 6 inches
Width over side sills .... 7 feet 0 inches
Width from under side of sill to trolley board .... 9 feet 1 inch
Height from top of rail to under side of sill .... 2 feet 9 inches
Height from top of rail to trolley board .... 11 feet 10 inches
Wheel base .... 8 feet 0 inches

CITY CARS

Straight Steel Sides; 22-Foot Body

This car, which is designed for double-end operation, ordinary method of fare collection, has sheet-steel sides. The underframe is of wood with drop platforms. The windows are arranged to drop into pockets. Seating capacity, 32 passengers. Interior finish golden oak. Equipped with radial drawbar and mounted on McGuire-Cummings A-1 suspension truck.

GENERAL DIMENSIONS

Length over all .... 31 feet 11 inches
Length over vestibule .... 31 feet 2 inches
Width over all .... 8 feet 3¼ inches
Width inside .... 7 feet 6 inches
Height from top of rail to underside of sill .... 2 feet 6 inches
Height from underside of sill to trolley board .... 9 feet 0 inches
Height from top of rail to trolley board .... 11 feet 6 inches
Wheel base .... 9 feet 0 inches

EXPRESS CARS

N THIS section are shown various types of baggage-express and express-freight cars we have built for interurban railroads. These cars however, are presented merely as typical of the many and various designs in cars of this character which we have constructed for all phases of electric railway service. As shown in the previous section, we build the combined passenger and baggage or express cars to serve various standard and special requirements. The cars shown in this section, however, are designed mainly for the transportation of express, package freight, merchandise, commodities, fruit, grain, produce, bulky material, vehicles and horses—freight which is generally sent by express owing to the necessity of quick transportation and careful handling both by electric and steam roads.

For large and bulky freight of this kind, the ordinary box car of the steam road would be the most practical and serviceable for electric railroads, but in most instances there is a pronounced objection by municipal authorities to the operation of freight cars through the streets.

In order to overcome this objection, we build these cars just as staunchly as the steam road box car but we modify the front and general exterior of the car so that it is acceptable to the public officials of the cities it traverses.

We build these cars for use both as trailers and motor cars. The motor express car is replacing the electric locomotive except for switching service.

For electric systems with steam road connections or where it is desired to "through" route a car over both electric and steam lines, we construct express cars complete with all equipment necessary to interchange with steam road service. This includes both automatic and straight air equipment, couplers of the radial type, running boards, side ladders and large or small end-doors.

In this connection we call your attention to the car described on page 42.

The tendency is to build express cars with composite underframes insuring great strength and the superstructure in proportion, to withstand the heavy load of a variable class of merchandise.

EXPRESS CARS

Trailer, Interchangeable with Steam Roads

Built to haul merchandise, grain and produce. It can be left on siding for loading and picked up the next morning loaded and sealed ready for through routing. All-wood underframe with cast-steel body bolsters. Equipped with McGuire-Cummings standard hand brakes and radial M. C. B. drawbar, and mounted on cast-steel, side-frame trucks.

GENERAL DIMENSIONS

Length over all	41 feet 5 inches
Length over vestibule	38 feet 9 inches
Width over all	9 feet 3 inches
Width inside	8 feet 5½ inches
Height from top of rail to under side of sill	3 feet 5 inches
Height from under side of sill to trolley board	9 feet 11 inches
Height from top of rail to trolley board	13 feet 4 inches
Truck centers	28 feet 6 inches
Wheel base	5 feet 2 inches

EXPRESS CARS

Motor Baggage Car for Way Service

This car was designed exclusively for electric railway operation, but with the idea of general utility in this service. It is in use as a way baggage car, its roominess permitting of the easy handling of heavy loads. When not in a regular run it is impressed into switching service. Underframe is of the composite type.

GENERAL DIMENSIONS

Length over all	52 feet 0 inches
Length over vestibule	39 feet 4 inches
Width over all	9 feet 3 inches
Width inside	8 feet 5 inches
Height from top of rail to under side of sill	3 feet 5 inches
Height from under side of sill to trolley board	9 feet 7 inches
Height from top of rail to trolley board	13 feet 0 inches
Truck centers	35 feet 0 inches
Wheel base	6 feet 6 inches

EXPRESS CARS

End Door Interchangeable Baggage Trail Car

Substantially built, especially adapted for heavy baggage service on both steam and electric roads. By means of the end doors, this car can be utilized for hauling material of extreme length, such as lumber, steel and other commodities. Underframe is of the composite type. Car is provided with side ladders and is equipped with McGuire-Cummings standard hand brakes and mounted on cast-steel side-frame trucks.

GENERAL DIMENSIONS

Length over all	41 feet 5 inches
Length over vestibule	38 feet 9 inches
Width over all	8 feet 11 inches
Width inside	8 feet 3½ inches
Height from top of rail to under side of sill	3 feet 5 inches
Height from under side of sill to trolley board	8 feet 11 inches
Height from top of rail to trolley board	12 feet 4 inches
Truck centers	28 feet 6 inches
Wheel base	5 feet 2 inches

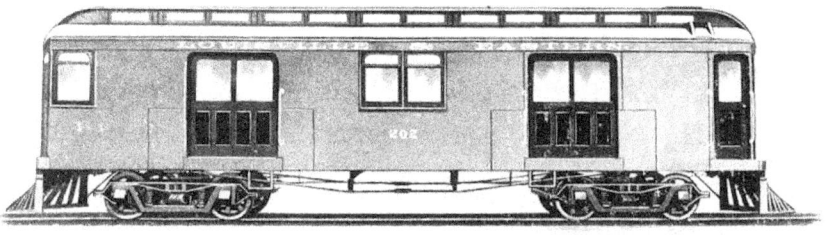

EXPRESS CARS

Quick Loading Motor Express Car

Two large side doors facilitate loading and unloading. This car was built to enable the quick transportation of package freight exclusively, irrespective of passenger runs, and was accordingly designed for double end operation and equipped with stationary locomotive pilot at each end. Has Monitor roof, composite underframe and is mounted on McGuire-Cummings No. 10-A, M. C. B. trucks.

GENERAL DIMENSIONS

Length over all	45 feet	0 inches
Length over vestibule	43 feet	8 inches
Width over all	8 feet	10 inches
Width inside	8 feet	2 inches
Height from top of rail to under side of sill	3 feet	0 inches
Height from under side of sill to trolley board	10 feet	3 inches
Height from top of rail to trolley board	13 feet	3 inches
Truck centers	28 feet	6 inches
Wheel base	6 feet	3 inches

EXPRESS CARS

Three-Door Motor Express —Freight Car

Utility, speed, quick loading and unloading, roominess, adaptability for trolley or third rail electric lines and for steam road service, either as a motor car or as a trail car—all these points are represented in this car. It is the practical embodiment of ideas covering several years of careful study into the requirements of this class of service.

The particular car shown, runs through a fruit belt, stopping at the principal loading platforms. It makes a remarkably quick run with its perishable freight to steamer docks, where direct loading into the boats is facilitated by the three large side doors.

There is a swinging door at each end and projecting running board on the roof for convenience of the train crew. The car has both automatic and straight air equipment and automatic couplers of the radial type. Mounted on McGuire-Cummings No. 20-A, M. C. B. trucks.

GENERAL DIMENSIONS

Length over all	50 feet	0 inches
Length over vestibule	49 feet	0 inches
Width over all	8 feet	10 inches
Width inside	8 feet	2½ inches
Height from top of rail to under side of sill	3 feet	5 inches
Height from under side of sill to trolley board	9 feet	4 inches
Height from top of rail to trolley board	12 feet	9 inches
Truck centers	31 feet	0 inches
Wheel base	6 feet	6 inches

EXPRESS CARS

Single End Motor Express Car

This car is designed as a combined express and motor car for hauling trailers. There is an exceedingly large side door which makes it possible to handle large and unwieldy express shipments in addition to ordinary way baggage.

Car is equipped with standard M. C. B. couplers and is mounted on McGuire-Cummings No. 20-A. M.C.B. trucks.

GENERAL DIMENSIONS

Length over all	50 feet 0 inches
Width over all	9 feet 0 inches
Width inside	8 feet 1 inch
Height from top of rail to under side of sill	3 feet 6 inches
Height from under side of sill to top of trolley board	8 feet 10 inches
Height from top of rail to trolley board	12 feet 4 inches
Truck centers	32 feet 0 inches
Wheel base	6 feet 6 inches

SPECIAL CARS

N THIS class of equipment we design and build cars for all phases of special service. As this subject is so broad, we have simply shown types of cars most commonly used to meet special service conditions. In designing these cars we have added to the usual construction a number of original features which have considerably increased the utility of the equipment in service. On the opposite page we show three types of substantially built freight cars which conform to all the requirements of steam road service making them thoroughly practical for use where an electric and steam road interchange equipment.

On page 46 we show a 200,000 pound capacity, 4-truck all-steel flat car, 70 feet 7 inches long, weighing 90,000 pounds. This car we built especially for the Santa Fe Railroad for hauling massive structural material. It is presented to illustrate the scope of our steel-car building facilities.

An electric locomotive, which has proven exceptionally economical in switching service, is shown on page 48.

Pages 50 and 51 illustrate crane cars we have constructed. We build these cars complete with cranes up to 16 tons capacity, or greater, if desired.

Pages 52 and 53 show fireproof, all-steel transformer cars, designed and built by this company.

In connection with the construction of special cars, the services of our engineers are at the disposal of our patrons in the designing of any desired type of equipment.

ELECTRIC SWITCHING LOCOMOTIVE

This locomotive has proven extremely economical for switching freight cars from industrial plants to main line tracks of steam road connections. It is equipped with M. C. B. couplers, straight and automatic air brake, and is mounted on McGuire-Cummings No. 10-A, M. C. B. trucks.

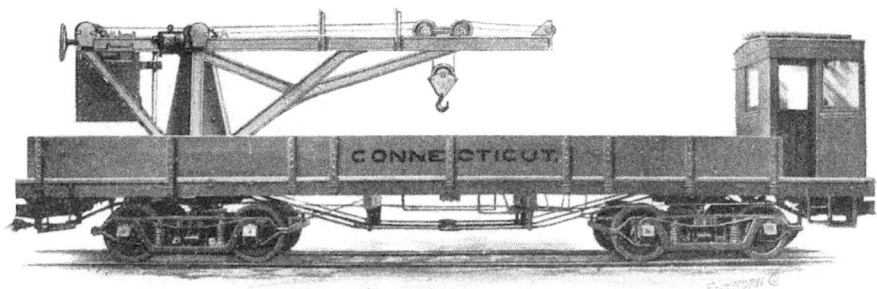

CRANE CAR EQUIPPED WITH 3-TON, 3-MOTOR PILLAR CRANE

This car is equipped with a 3-motor electric pillar crane with a capacity of 3 tons. The effective radius is 18 feet. Extreme radius, 20 feet 3 inches. Distance from high point of hook to base of pillar, 3 feet 8 inches. Height of crane, 7 feet 3½ inches. Equipped with 550 volt direct current motors; 11 H. P. motor for hoisting, giving a speed of 15 feet per minute; 2 H. P. motor for rotating, giving a speed of 1½ revolutions per minute, and 2 H. P. for trolley travel, giving a speed of about 40 feet per minute.

Crane is furnished with counterbalance box located back of the mast, thereby lifting the 3 ton load at 18 feet radius at right angles to line of track without blocking up or fastening car to rails.

Crane is provided with cast iron pillar supporting steel frame work. Pillar at top is surmounted with commutator, thus allowing crane to rotate in a complete circle.

Steel wire hoisting rope is used. Car is mounted on McGuire-Cummings No. 10-A, M. C. B. trucks.

SUB-STATION CAR

Built of Steel. Eliminates Fire Risk

The sub-station car, illustrated, was constructed entirely of steel, in order to eliminate the danger of fire, which has frequently resulted in total loss of valuable electrical apparatus, as well as destruction of cars when wooden sub-station cars have been used.

The cost of the steel car may run approximately 10 per cent greater than wooden, but the advantages are tremendously in favor of the all-metal type.

These cars are built either as trail or motor cars. The ends of the car are removable to enable the installation of the electrical equipment. The section of roof over the transformer is removable to enable the replacement of parts, etc. The end transoms open full depth, to insure proper ventilation. Car is mounted on standard M. C. B. freight car trucks.

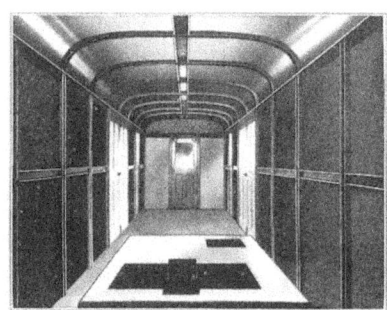

GENERAL DIMENSIONS

Length over all	40 feet 0 inches
Width over all	8 feet 1 inch
Width inside	7 feet 10 inches
Height from top of rail to under side of sill	3 feet 0 inches
Height from top of rail to top of roof	13 feet 0 inches
Height from underside of sill to roof	10 feet 0 inches
Truck centers	27 feet 0 inches

SUB-STATION CAR

Thirty-four feet long. Constructed throughout of steel, rendering the car proof against fire. Similar in design to car described on opposite page.

SUB-STATION CAR

Forty feet in length. All steel construction. Absolutely fireproof. Same general design as car described on opposite page.

SUB-STATION CAR

Forty feet in length. Built of steel, eliminating all danger of fire damage to electrical apparatus or to car. Designed along the same general lines as car described on opposite page.

20

TRUCKS

cGUIRE-CUMMINGS Trucks, the triumph of a quarter of a century of development, represent the highest expression of accumulated experience and inventive skill. From the day of its inception, it has been a fixed policy with this company to keep its product representative of the best and most progressive in truck building. How well that policy has been adhered to is evidenced by gold medal awards of the World's Fair in Chicago, Pan-American Exposition at Buffalo, and the World's Fair at St. Louis—the highest honors ever extended to a truck builder.

There is no part of a car more important than its trucks. Upon the trucks depend the safety and comfort of passengers, as well as the efficiency and economy of the rolling stock.

True value of a car, of course, must be determined by the character of the product as a whole. It must be tested by its all-around capacity, and not by a special or selected feature. But of all the parts of a car the trucks primarily should represent the highest development of engineering skill and workmanship.

While economy in the cost of truck construction is regarded by railways in numerous instances as a prime essential, economy is by no means a dominant idea of this company in the building of its trucks. Certainly not the economy of mere cheapness.

Safety, strength, long life, efficiency and low maintenance cost in service are the "economy factors" entering into the construction of McGuire-Cummings trucks. On the other hand, however, notwithstanding the highest attainable point of mechanical perfection characterizing our trucks, we can build them at prices that make them truly economical viewed from the standpoint of both first cost and ultimate economy resulting from their long service and low maintenance expense.

This is made possible because of our extensive truck building facilities—our forge shop and truck department being one of the largest and best equipped in the United States.

A few representative trucks among the thousands we have built for all classes of electric railway service are shown in this section.

McGUIRE-CUMMINGS
SOLID STEEL COLUMBIAN SINGLE TRUCK

A Durable Truck of Simple Design for City Cars
(Patented)

This truck has fewer parts than any design on the market. The side frames are made in one piece including all spring cups, and are supported on two cushion springs over each journal box. Spring seats cast on box and caps cast in frame. By the use of three-quarter elliptic and spiral springs, an extra long spring base is made possible, insuring easy riding. The journal boxes are dust-proof. Brakes are double-acting and equipped with McGuire-Cummings patented "Elastic" brake hanger, which automatically takes up its own wear and absolutely prevents giving of brake. Wheel base can be varied to meet requirements.

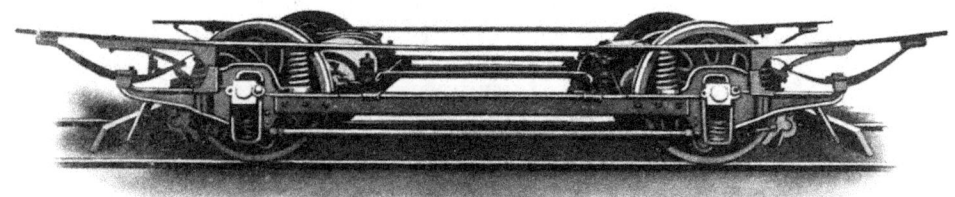

McGUIRE-CUMMINGS
A-1 SUSPENSION SINGLE TRUCK

An Exceptionally Easy-Riding Truck for City Cars
(Patented)

On this truck the car body is carried very low. The spring base is extended 4 feet at each end beyond the wheel base, by means of extension elliptic springs and this prevents longitudinal oscillation. Frame is supported on cushion springs, mounted on swinging links, which eliminate the jolt and jar and make it the steadiest and easiest-riding truck on the market. The journal boxes are dust-proof. Brakes are double acting and provided with McGuire-Cummings patented "Elastic" brake hanger. The simplicity and durability of this truck reduce the cost of maintenance to a minimum.

McGUIRE-CUMMINGS
No. 10-A, M. C. B. DOUBLE TRUCK

A Built-up Truck for City and Suburban Cars

Built up of structural steel and wrought iron. Cast pedestals. Double elliptic bolster springs. Double coil, equalizing springs. Journals 4¼ x 8 inches. All parts machine-fitted. This truck has met with great favor throughout the country owing to its simplicity of design, strength, durability and light weight. There is no maintenance expense except for wheels and brake shoes. More than 1,000 trucks of this type have been sold by this company in Chicago alone.

McGUIRE-CUMMINGS
No. 20-A, M. C. B. DOUBLE TRUCK

Particularly Adapted For Heavy Interurban Service

Built up of wrought iron and structural steel. Cast pedestals. Has equalizing springs and bolster springs of the double elliptic type. Journals 4½ x 8 inches. Forged steel side-frames. Machine-fitted throughout. A strong, easy-riding truck which will reduce maintenance expense to a minimum.

McGUIRE-CUMMINGS
No. 70-A HIGH SPEED DOUBLE TRUCK

A Heavy Forged Truck for Interurban Service

M. C. B. truck, specially designed for high speed interurban service. Has double coil equalizing springs, insuring easy riding qualities. Triple elliptic bolster springs. This truck has reinforced end sill and large steel transom gusset plates, keeping the truck rigid and in true at all times. Side frames are of forged steel. All parts machine-fitted. This truck represents maximum efficiency, minimum cost of maintenance, and superior riding qualities.

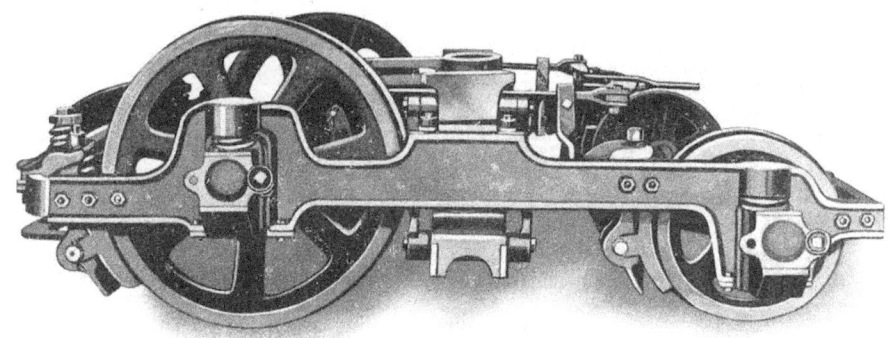

McGUIRE-CUMMINGS
MAXIMUM TRACTION DOUBLE TRUCK

A Single Motor Truck Adapted Especially for City Cars

This type of truck with a single motor feature means a saving in weight for city cars. The truck itself with its pony wheels constitutes one of the lightest bolster trucks made, and the use of but one motor reduces the weight of truck equipment materially.

Has solid steel frame with patent springs over journal boxes and swing bolster on elliptic and spiral springs. An exceptionally easy-riding truck.

McGUIRE-CUMMINGS
No. 39-A CAST STEEL DOUBLE TRUCK

Outside-Hung Motor Truck for City Service
(Patented)

Has a solid steel side frame. Four cushion coil-springs over each journal box. Solid steel swing bolster mounted on elliptic and spiral springs. Each truck has 22 springs or 44 to the car, properly proportioned, giving easy spring movement. Carries car nearly as low as a single truck. Short wheel base, outside-hung motors. All parts machine-fitted. Particularly adapted for short radius curves. Strongest truck made in proportion to weight.

McGUIRE-CUMMINGS
No. 29-D TRUCK for ELEVATED ROADS

A Strong and Durable Truck for Elevated Service

Cast steel one-piece side frame. Cast steel bolsters. Double elliptic bolster springs. Cushion coil springs on each side of the journal boxes. All parts machine-fitted. A truck which has gained great favor with the elevated railways because of its strength, durability and low maintenance cost in service.

SNOW SWEEPERS AND PLOWS

S PIONEERS in the development and construction of snow fighting equipment we present the following snow sweepers and plows confident in the assertion that they are not surpassed, if indeed equaled, in efficiency by any similar machines on the market. The first long-broom snow sweeper with rotary brushes ever constructed in this country was built by this company years ago, at a time when primitive hand shovel methods of removing snow from electric railways were in vogue and the highly developed labor and expense-saving snow sweepers and plows of the present day had not been conceived of. While of course this first machine lacked many of the important features characterizing our present designs it proved a tremendous step in advance and awakened railway officials to the fact that lines could be kept open regardless of the fall of snow and enormous savings in time, labor and dollars and cents could be effected by the use of mechanical equipment of this kind. From that time on this company has been foremost in developing this important class of equipment, so that today McGuire-Cummings snow plows and sweepers are acknowledged as pre-eminent in electric railway service throughout the world. The same high standards of mechanical perfection and practical utility characterizing the various products of this company shaped the construction of McGuire-Cummings snow fighting equipment and the efficiency of the machines is attested by the fact that more than 1400 machines are in use on fully 90 per cent of the electric railways in the United States and Canada which have snow to contend with.

The various designs shown are described in detail including the manner in which the combination sweeper may be used the year around—in winter for the removal of snow and during the other eight or nine months as a baggage, express or work car.

The quality of rattan used and the ease of refilling the sweeper brooms when worn out, is described on page 92.

**Underframing Entirely of Steel.
Brooms Extend 15 inches on the Outside of Each Track.
Instantaneous Wheel and Lever Control of
Sweeping Mechanism**

SNOW SWEEPERS

Standard Single Truck Sweeper with Long Brooms
(U. S. and Canadian Patents)

This machine is 28 feet 3 inches in length over all, 7 feet in width over the cab, and 10 feet 7 inches in height from the top of the rail to the top of the cab. The cab is straight vestibule type as shown in the engraving. The machine is built to suit any gauge of track. The underframing is entirely of steel, the side sills being of 8-inch "I" beams. End sills of 8-inch channels, and the cross beams of 6-inch channels, diagonally braced with angles and held together at the corners with suitable gussets and heavy corner bands, all being riveted together with $\frac{5}{8}$-inch and $\frac{3}{4}$-inch rivets.

The brooms are 32 inches in diameter, filled with best grade rattan, and made in four segments each. The broom driving shaft, located inside the cab, is of a diameter to suit motor used. The broom pedestals are of malleable iron. Brooms are raised and lowered by means of hand wheels, which are conveniently located on the inside of the cab. The side plows are built up of $\frac{1}{4}$-inch steel, the standard being 24 inches in height and 6 feet 6 inches in length, and arranged to raise and lower 8 inches, and to clear a space of four feet on the outside of the rail. They are designed for instantaneous operation by means of hand wheels and

(Continued From Previous Page)

levers on the inside of the cab. Sand boxes are of manufacturer's standard design and located in diagonal corners of the car.

This machine is exceptionally rigid. The ends of the car projecting beyond the truck are substantially braced with pipe braces, extending from the journal box pedestal to the diagonal corners of the underframe, as illustrated. The trucks are of the pedestal type using the standard 33-inch cast iron wheel, of a tread and flange and gauge of track to suit. Axles are of open hearth steel, and are keyseated to suit the motors which may be specified. The brakes, of jam-tight design, are connected to the brake staffs located in each end of the car. It requires two 25-H. P. motors to propel the car, and one 25 to 30-H. P. motor to operate the brooms. This machine weighs complete, without electrical equipment, approximately 20,000 pounds.

**Perspective View
of Sweeper Illustrated on
Opposite Page**

This shows the method of holding the brooms in the pedestals, the method of raising and lowering them, the easy access to the broom journal and the method of removing the brooms when it is necessary for refilling the same with rattan. It also illustrates the relation of the diagonal end sills to the broom, which prevents the snow from packing under the car body.

**End View of
Sweeper Illustrated on
Opposite Page**

Showing the broom extending across the rails, and fifteen inches on the outside of each track.

SNOW SWEEPERS

Standard Double Truck Combination Long Broom Sweeper, Baggage, Express and Work Car

Brooms and sweeping mechanism designed and constructed so that when not in use, they can be removed with ease, thus converting the car into a straight baggage, express or work car.

Double Truck, Long Broom Sweeper—Steel Underframe
(Patented)

The utility and economy of this Combination Snow Sweeper and Baggage, Express and Work Car are obvious. It is adaptable for service in all seasons of the year. Length is 53 feet over the broom beams, and width over all is 8 feet 5 inches. The car body over the buffers, with the brooms removed, when used as a work car is 39 feet 7⅞ inches in length. The trucks are spaced 22 feet 6 inches from center to center. The underframing of the car is entirely of structural steel, sills being 9-inch "I" beams; buffers 7 inch by 3½-inch angles, bent to a suitable form. The frame is braced diagonally, making the same very rigid and strong. The super-structure of the car is of wood, of standard baggage car construction. Car is sheathed both inside and out. Roofing is of the "turtle deck" type, covered with No. 8 cotton duck, and equipped with standard type trolley board. Broom and broom-driving mechanism, pedestals and side plows are identical with that on Standard Single Truck Sweeper, illustrated and described in the two following pages.

Double Truck Sweeper as Baggage and Express Car

Top View of Broom Segment Showing Simple Method of Refilling Brooms

RATTAN

The Highest Grade Imported from Singapore is Used in the McGuire-Cummings Sweepers

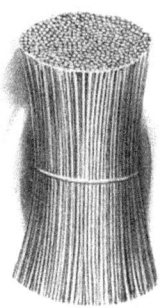

The rattan used for McGuire-Cummings snow sweepers is of the highest grade possible to obtain. It is imported at the beginning of each season direct from Singapore. Only rattan of carefully selected quality capable of withstanding severe service is utilized. This rattan is carried on hand in large quantities cut to 32 inch lengths and also in natural lengths for the benefit of patrons with special requirements.

Illustrations show the manner in which McGuire-Cummings brooms are constructed; also the ease with which the brooms can be refilled. When the rattan becomes worn, it is removed by simply taking the segment from the broom shaft and pulling out the rattan from the underside. The new rattan is then placed in the brooms by taking a sufficient number of pieces to fill one of the holes, bending the same double in the middle, lacing it through another hole and then pounding it down tight on the back, as shown in the upper illustration at the left.

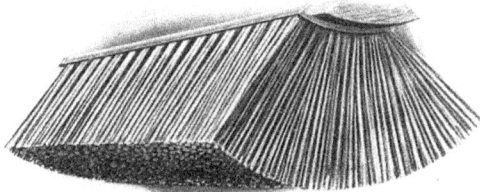

End Perspective View of Broom Segment. There are Four Segments to Each Broom

Broom Back

SNOW PLOWS

Standard Single Truck Shear Plow

This plow which is designed for both city and interurban work is one of the most efficient snow fighting devices built. It is especially adapted for work where snows are frequent and drifts accumulate 2 to 4 feet deep. Operates in both directions. Constructed also in double truck design.

Can be Used Also as a Work Car or Locomotive

Particular attention has been paid to insure proper angle in setting the shear, and the proper curve to the plow, so as to require the least possible power for propelling.

The side wing, which is illustrated, is arranged to raise and lower by means of a hand lever as illustrated in the engraving at the right.

Underframing of the car is rigidly constructed of long leaf yellow pine sills, reinforced with suitable steel channels. The car body proper is arranged so that the car can be used for a work car or locomotive. The truck is of the pedestal design, having springs on each side of the journal box. The construction of the truck is arranged so that it can be made for any gauge of track. The wheels are 33 inches diameter and of the required tread and flange which may be specified. Owing to the shape of the plow, the power required for propulsion is reduced to a minimum. The car illustrated is equipped with two 25-H. P. motors.

SNOW PLOWS

Standard Double Truck Combination Nose Plow and Baggage Car

Can be Converted into Straight Baggage Car by Simply Removing the Plows

The body of the car is of standard baggage car construction, of dimensions as may be specified, and arranged for the application of the nose plow. The nose plow illustrated is 4 feet in height and designed to clean a space 10 feet in width without the use of the side wings. The nose is constructed to raise and lower by means of worm gear and hand wheel. Also built for air operation. The spread of the side wings, is adjusted by means of hand wheel and levers from the inside of the car to any desired height and at any angle, at will of the operator. This combination is designed so that the plow mechanism can be easily removed, thus converting the car into a straight baggage or express car free from obstruction on the inside of the car, caused by the removal of these parts.

OPERATED AS A FIRE ENGINE
McGuire-Cummings Standard 4,000 Gallon Pneumatic Sprinkler Throwing a Stream From a Standard Fire Nozzle Over a Building 45 Feet High

PNEUMATIC SPRINKLER

4,000 Gallon Capacity
Double Truck
Sprinkler
(Patented)

A number of these machines, in use in Chicago, are rendering excellent service. This sprinkler is of a standard design, approved by the Chicago Board of Supervising Engineers.

It is used for sprinkling the right of way or street up to 100 feet in width, or any distance up to 50 feet each side of the center line of the track.

This machine is designed and built on the most scientific principles. The frame work of the car is built entirely of structural steel and assembled in the most rigid manner.

The water compartment of the tank is of ¼-inch steel with ⅜-inch heads. The air compartment is of ⅜-inch steel with 7/16-inch heads. The compressor supplying the air is of the standard independent electric driven air brake type, water cooled and of an approved make, of ample capacity to maintain a pressure of 80 to 90 pounds on the air reservoir. This is controlled by means of an automatic governor.

(Continued From Previous Page)

The pressure in the water reservoir is regulated by means of a reducing valve which is adjustable to any desired pressure ranging from 2 to 20 pounds. This apparatus is automatic and requires no attention during the operation.

For localities where the water supply is not readily accessible, this car can be equipped with a centrifugal filling pump, driven by a connection from the compressor motor, and arranged in such a manner as to permit the filling of the tank from streams along the side of or adjacent to the right of way.

At the right is given a table of calculations which are based on actual tests with sprinkling car operated at a speed of 12 miles per hour with the water under a pressure of 20 pounds.

PNEUMATIC SPRINKLER

4,000 Gallon
Capacity
Double Truck
Sprinkler
(Patented)

Capacity, Gallons	Type of Truck	DIMENSIONS OVER ALL			Weight Without Electric Equipment	Weight of Electric Equipment	Weight of Water	Weight Complete	Distance Sprinkling Right of Way Only	Distance Sprinkling Entire Width of Street
		Length	Width	Height						
3000	Single	25' 6"	7' 6"	10' 6"	18000	5400	25000	48200	6 Miles	2½ Miles
4000	Double	29' 6"	7' 6"	10' 6"	24300	10400	33300	68000	7 Miles	3½ Miles
4500	Double	32'	7' 6"	10' 6"	25400	10400	37500	73300	8 Miles	4 Miles
5000	Double	34'	7' 6"	10' 6"	25850	10400	42000	78250	9 Miles	4½ Miles
6000	Double	37'	10' 6"	10' 6"	26800	10400	50000	87200	11 Miles	5½ Miles

PNEUMATIC SPRINKLER

3,000 Gallon Capacity, Single Truck Sprinkler
(Patented)

SNOW PLOWS

Combination Snow Plow, Pneumatic Sprinkler, Line Car, Sand Car and Locomotive

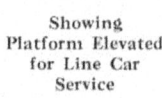

Showing Platform Elevated for Line Car Service

This machine is a combination of a snow plow, pneumatic sprinkler, line car, sand car and electric locomotive. For line car purposes it has a platform over the rear cab, which is arranged to elevate to a distance of 20 feet from the top of rail. This platform measures 4 feet by 8 feet. The raising and lowering of this platform is controlled by a winch located inside the cab.

The sprinkling mechanism is of standard design, and operated in the same manner as that of the standard pneumatic sprinkler.

The plow arrangement is designed so that the raising and lowering mechanism, the plow beams and plows, can be easily removed in the summer season when it is desired to use the car in sprinkler service.

The car is equipped with standard M. C. B. couplers and can be used in connection with steam railroad equipment. It is equipped with four 500 volt, 90-H. P. motors.

Under the water tanks of this car are steel reservoirs, or boxes, for holding sand, salt and line materials.

The air sanding device is mounted on the front end sill of each truck instead of on the body of the car.

Car is mounted on McGuire-Cummings No. 20-A, M. C. B. trucks. When used as an electric locomotive, car weighs approximately 112,000 pounds.

IN PRESENTING this general catalogue of electric railway equipment, we desire primarily to direct your attention to our extensive car building facilities. With plants centrally located, both at Chicago and Paris, Ill., equipped with the most modern machinery, operated under the careful direction of competent Superintendents and Engineers, and backed by a quarter of a century's experience, we are prepared to construct efficiently and promptly, all classes of rolling stock for the successful operation of electric railways.

It has been the policy of the management of this company at all times and at whatever cost, to keep its products representative of that which is best and most progressive, and to adhere strictly to the plans and specifications in the building of equipment. Numerous re-orders from many of the largest electric railways attest their satisfaction with the material and class of workmanship entering into the construction of our equipment.

Our Chicago plant has connections with all the railroads entering Chicago, and our Paris, Ill., plant is situated on the Vandalia-Pennsylvania System, the St. Louis Division of the "Big Four" New York Central lines, and the Cairo Division of the "Big Four" New York Central lines; also connects with the Terre Haute, Indianapolis & Eastern Railway (electric).

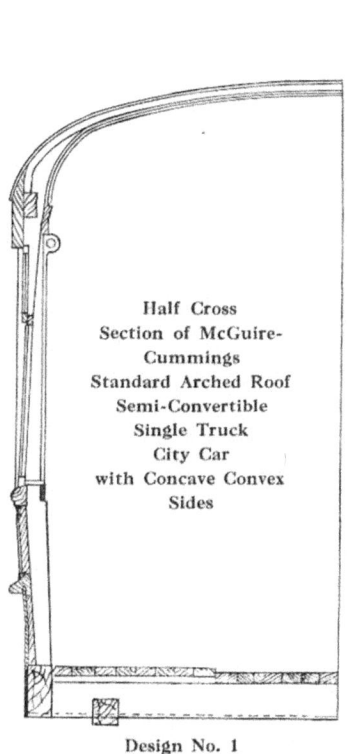

Half Cross Section of McGuire-Cummings Standard Arched Roof Semi-Convertible Single Truck City Car with Concave Convex Sides

Design No. 1

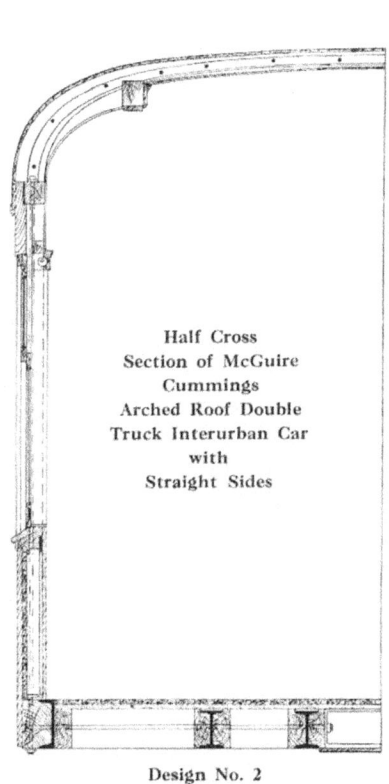

Half Cross Section of McGuire-Cummings Arched Roof Double Truck Interurban Car with Straight Sides

Design No. 2

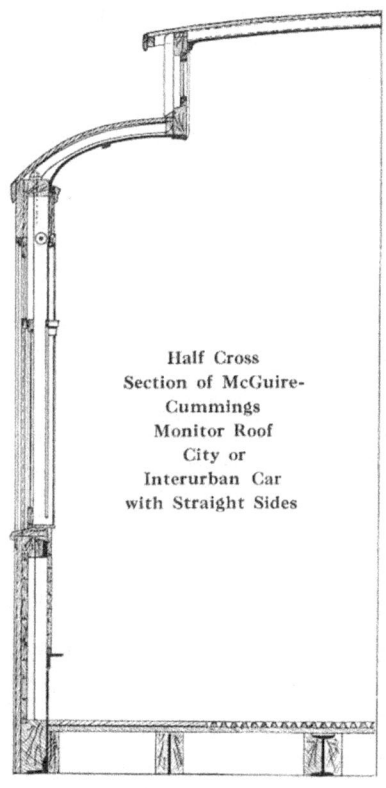

Half Cross Section of McGuire-Cummings Monitor Roof City or Interurban Car with Straight Sides

Design No. 3

Specify These
For Your
New Cars

ELECTRIC SERVICE SUPPLIES CO.
Manufacturer of
Railway Material and Electrical Supplies

PHILADELPHIA	NEW YORK	CHICAGO
17th and Cambria Streets	Hudson Terminal	417 South Dearborn Street

The car equipment illustrated herein is listed and described in detail in Our Supplement to, and in, Car Equipment Catalog No. 4, Vol. 2. A copy is yours for the asking.

Form ME-255

PRINTED BY
ALFRED M. SLOCUM CO.
718-724 ARCH ST.
PHILA.

KEYSTONE  QUALITY

Union Standard Ball Bearing Trolley Base No. 14

Union Standard Ball Bearing Trolley Base No. 11

Union Standard Trolley Bases, in both roller and ball bearing types, have all wearing parts, including the base pin, swivel and socket axle pin, made from special high carbon steel. Rollways and sleeves in which balls and rollers operate are made of carbon seamless steel, and are easily removable.

The complete line is listed in Catalog No. 4, Vol. 2 and Supplement to same.

Keystone Trolley Catcher

Catalog No. 18766 Keystone Trolley Catcher. A simple machine of few parts and one that positively will not rebound. Keystone Trolley Catchers are made to fit sockets used by the Earll, Wilson and Ideal trolley catchers, also the Earll and Knutson retrievers, permitting the maintenance of any type of sockets that may have been adopted as a standard.

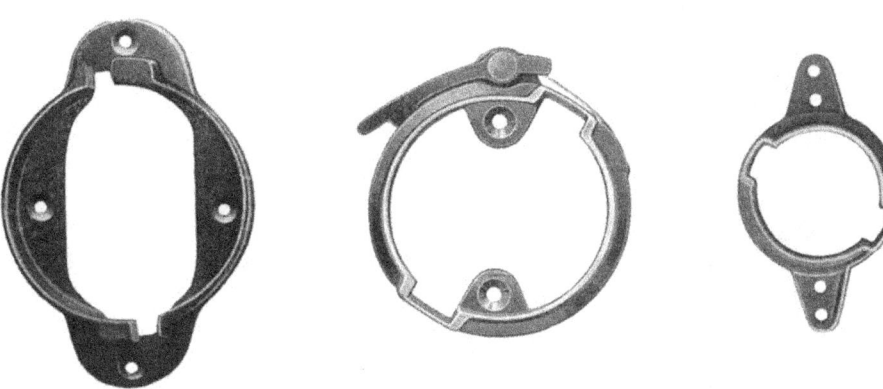

Trolley Catcher Sockets

Samson "Spot" Trolley, Bell and Register Cord

KEYSTONE QUALITY

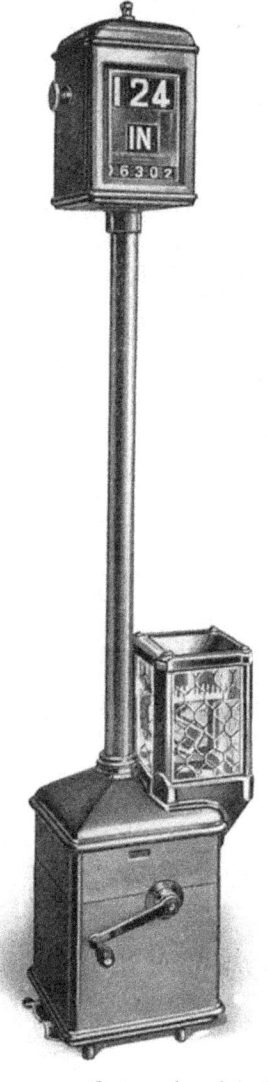

International Coin Registers

Proven to be the ideal method for collecting and registering fares on Prepayment Cars, combining as they do, all the features of a fare box, a coin counting machine and a car register.

Fares are dropped in the box, either in nickels, dimes or pennies. They are counted by the machine, delivered into the conductor's receptacle and so made available for change. The counting mechanism operates the car register through the upright column, advancing the trip register one fare and the totalizer five cents for each nickel or five pennies counted, or two fares and ten cents for each dime counted.

The fare box shown above is similar to the coin register except that no car register is attached.

The totalizer is mounted just above the money-counting mechanism where it can be plainly seen by passengers paying fares or by inspectors entering or leaving the car. The figures are ½ inch high and read in dollars and cents.

KEYSTONE QUALITY

International Fare Registers
Single and Double Types

Single Connector Applied to Leather Cord

Single Leather
Connector

Double Connector Applied to Cotton Cord

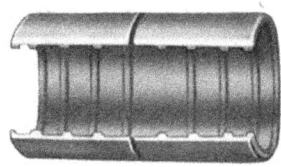

Double Leather Connector

Single Cotton Connector

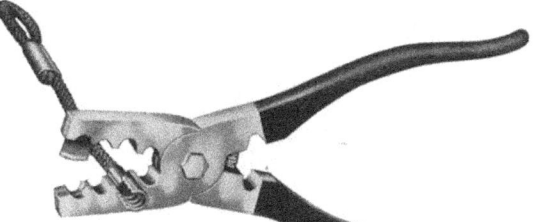

Combination Pliers for Attaching

Double Cotton
Connector

Keystone Cord Connectors—For Trolley, Bell
and Register Cord

KEYSTONE  QUALITY

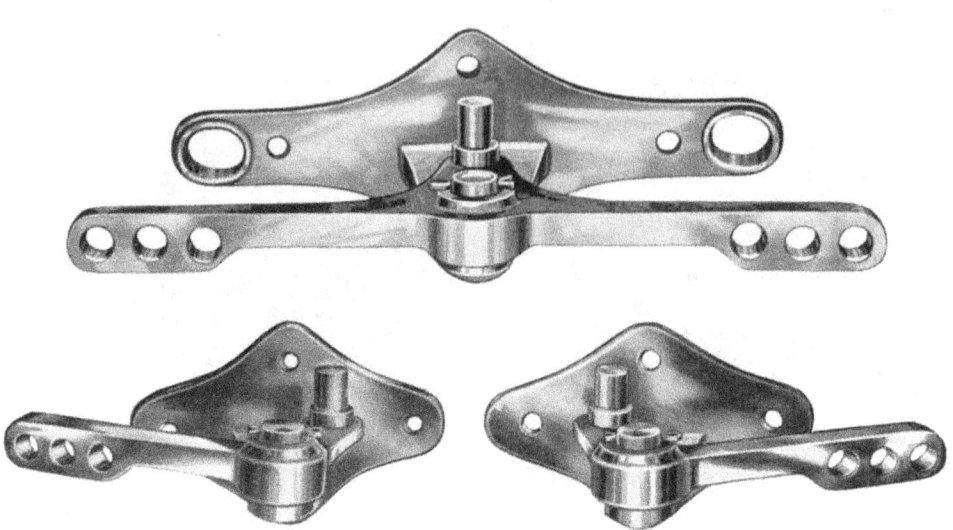

Fare Register Cord Pull Devices

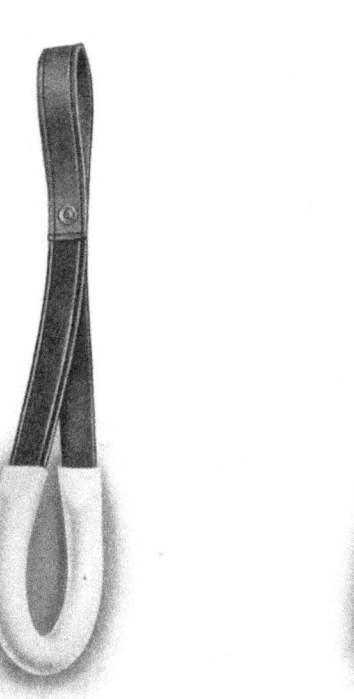

Sanitary Hand Straps

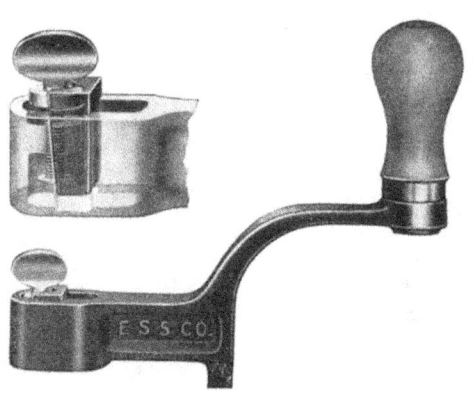

"Lock-On" Controller Handle

A controller handle that *locks* to the shaft, thereby overcoming the great troubles caused by loosely fitting controller handles.

They prevent wear of both the controller handle and shaft as well as preventing destructive arcing inside the controller due to improper lining up of the contacts, both of which are caused by loosely fitting handles.

They have an adjustment of ⅛ inch, so fitting new or badly worn shafts, and making them interchangeable on all controllers of a given type.

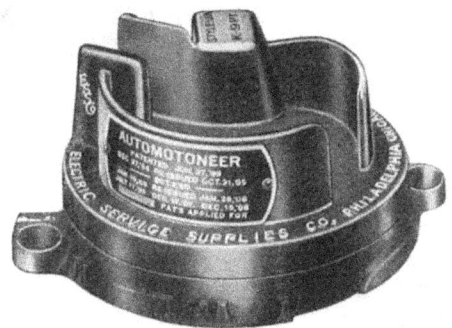

The Automotoneer

A device for "Controlling the Controller." It compels the motorman to stop at each point during the forward movement of the controller handle, thereby allowing the motors time to properly accelerate.

The Automotoneer *enforces* proper controller operation; cuts down maintenance on motors, controllers, gears, pinions and entire equipment, fifteen to forty per cent. Reduces peak starting loads 25 to 40 per cent.

Made for all standard railway controllers, as well as for many mine and industrial types.

KEYSTONE  QUALITY

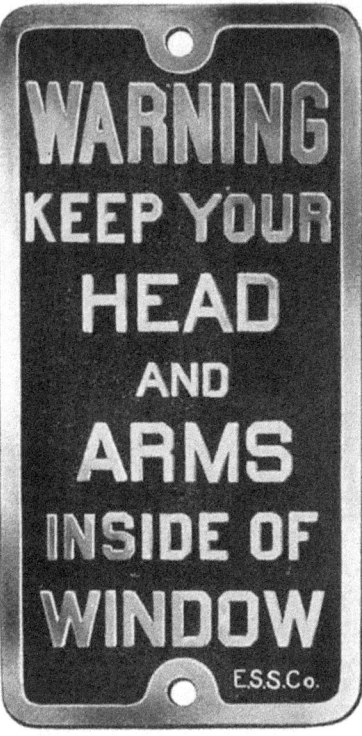

Keystone Brass and Enamelled Signs, Cap and Coat Badges

KEYSTONE  QUALITY

Portable "GOLDEN GLOW" Headlight for Interurban Service

Portable "GOLDEN GLOW" Headlight for Suburban Service

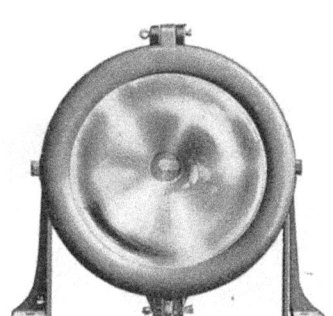 

Hood or Roof Type "GOLDEN GLOW" Headlight

"GOLDEN GLOW" incandescent headlights are supplied in pressed steel cases, with polished and ground mirrored glass reflectors of high efficiency, which cannot be scratched, burned or tarnish. The gold color of the glass absorbs the violet rays, resulting in a reduced amount of glare and a greater amount of penetration when the air is full of dust or moisture.

KEYSTONE QUALITY

"GOLDEN GLOW" Headlight—Flush Type

"GOLDEN GLOW" Headlight—Semi-Flush Type

"GOLDEN GLOW" Headlight—Surface Type

"GOLDEN GLOW" headlights for mounting on or in the dash are made with pressed steel cases in the three types as illustrated above and with plain or grid doors. They are all equipped with the well known "GOLDEN GLOW" mirrored glass reflectors as described on the opposite page.

KEYSTONE QUALITY

No. 19402 Resistance Panel
Containing Removable Resistance Unit and Enclosed Fuse

No. 19403   Buzzer

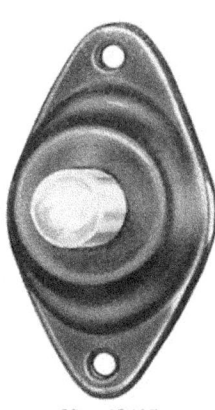

No. 19405
Standard Push Button

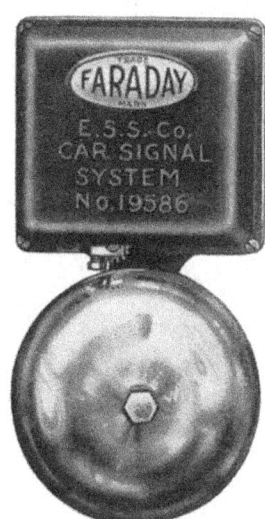

No. 19586
Single Stroke Bell

No. 19585   Extra Loud Buzzer

Faraday high voltage car signal system offers an economical and dependable means of operating passenger signals or motormen's door signals direct from the trolley circuit, thus doing away with the troublesome, costly and undependable dry cell battery. Any number of buttons may be installed in a car and signals may be made by means of standard buzzers or single stroke or vibrating bells. Various types of push buttons are also available.

KEYSTONE QUALITY

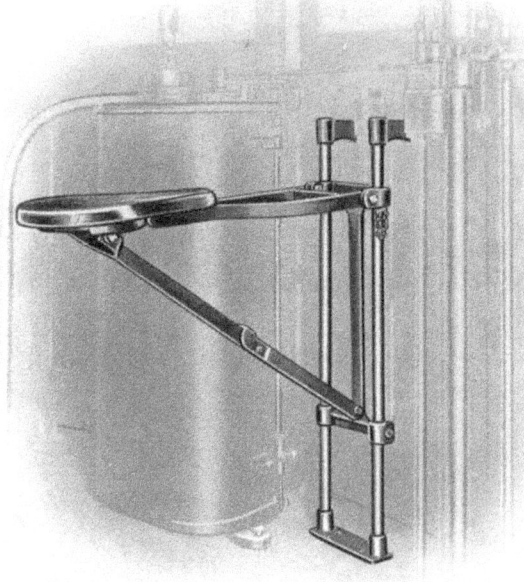

Keystone Motorman's Seat—Stationary Type

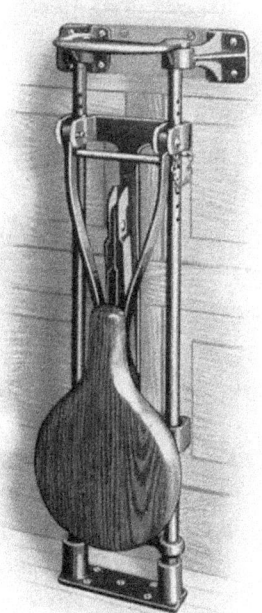

Keystone motormen's seats are instantly collapsible and adjustable and are made in stationary or portable form. They are also supplied as conductors' seats for attachment to standard control stands.

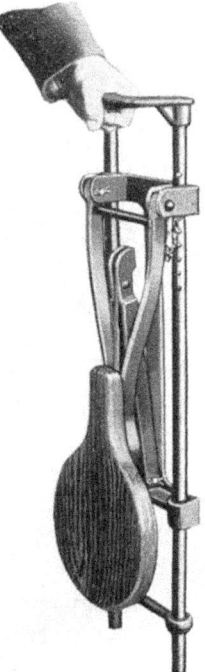

Keystone Motorman's Seat—Removable Type

KEYSTONE  QUALITY

Keystone Car Sign—Type I
Installed above Vestibule Window

Keystone Car Sign—Type S

Keystone Car Sign—Type I

The curtain roller form of sign is generally recognized as the best means of designating a route or the destination of cars both from the viewpoint of the public and that of the railway operator.

They permit of great flexibility in operation due to the fact that all of the destinations required on a system or a division of a system may usually be carried on one curtain. The curtains, showing white letters on a black background, are highly legible in daylight and equally so at night time when illuminated from the rear.

KEYSTONE QUALITY

Keystone Route Sign—Type H

Keystone Route Number Sign—Type S

Hunter Route Number Sign—Type No. 6, Double Face

Curtain signs are supplied in complete pressed steel glazed boxes as illustrated, also in steel frames for installation in a box provided as part of the car. Where conditions require curtains without frames or boxes, curtains alone may be furnished.

KEYSTONE QUALITY

Hunter Side Window Sign—Type No. 16

Hunter Side Window Sign—Rear View

Hunter Route and Destination Sign—Type No. 17

Curtain signs are made to meet all conditions; for installation in the front vestibule windows, in the side windows, on the roof, in the monitor windows or on the dash.

KEYSTONE  QUALITY

"Safety" Car Fixture with Opal Reflector

"Safety" Fixture
Sectional View

"Safety" Fixture—Cover Removed

Modern car lighting calls for the use of proper fixtures and reflectors from a standpoint of appearance, economy in operation and general satisfaction to the riding public.

"Safety" fixtures in combination with Mazda lamps and properly designed reflectors uniformly distribute the light where needed and show a material saving in current consumption.

"Safety" fixtures are made in straight and angle base, pendant and bracket forms for use with all standard combinations of Mazda lamps and reflectors.

KEYSTONE QUALITY

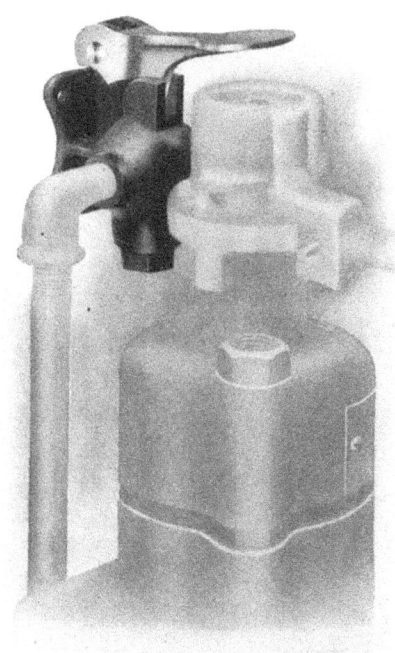

Showing Application of Keystone Single Valve, over Engineer's Brake Valve

Keystone "Leakless" Valve—Double Type

Keystone "Leakless" Valve—Foot Type

Armored Type Air Pipe—Insulating Joint

Keystone Trailer Connectors and Sockets

The Exposed Ends are "Dead" when the Connector is Pulled Apart

K E Y S T O N E Q U A L I T Y

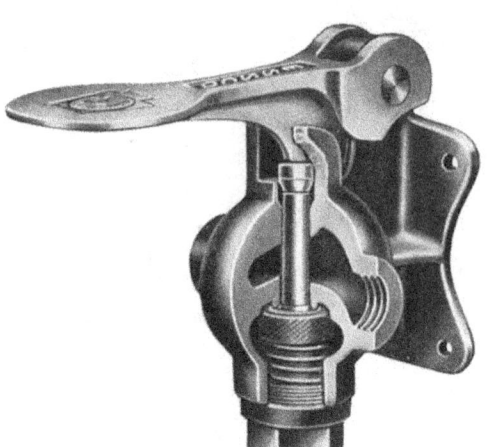

Keystone "Leakless" Valves—Single Types

Air Pipe Fittings

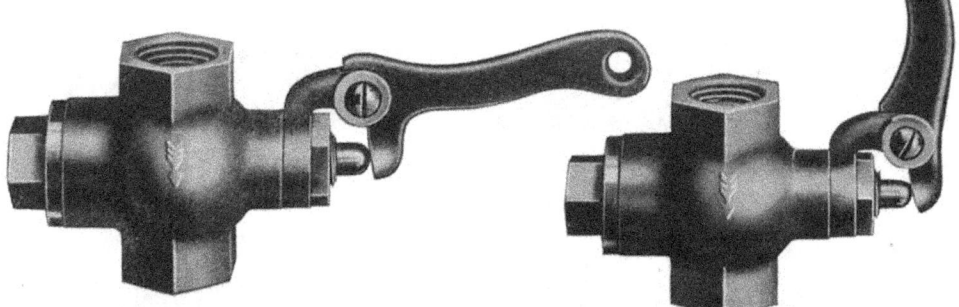

Keystone "Leakless" Valves—Whistle Types

KEYSTONE QUALITY

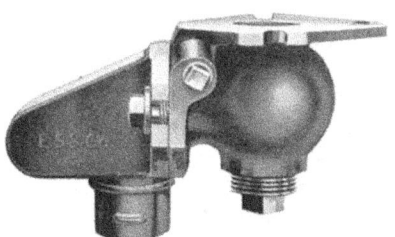 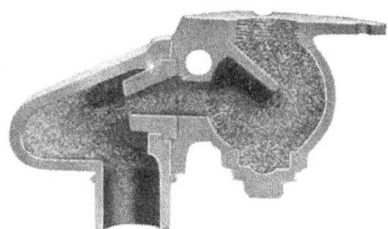

Keystone Vacuum Sanders

Keystone Air Sanders

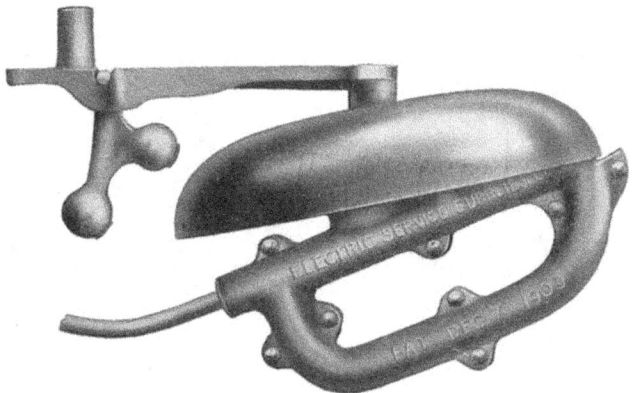

Keystone Pneumatic Gong Ringer—Installed

KEYSTONE QUALITY

Forged Steel Gears and Pinions

Blanks for these are forged under tremendous pressure, so have great density and consequent freedom from defects. This means exceptional wearing qualities.

They have less weight than regular cast steel gears, better balance, more uniform design as well as higher physical properties and freedom from shrinkage holes.

Furnished for all standard motors of modern design.

Garton-Daniels
Lightning Arresters

Recording Car Meters
Watt-Hour and Ampere-Hour Types

KEYSTONE  QUALITY

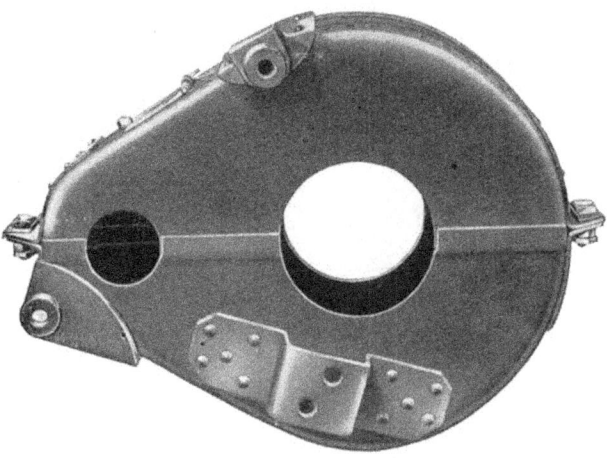

For General Electric 203-A Motor

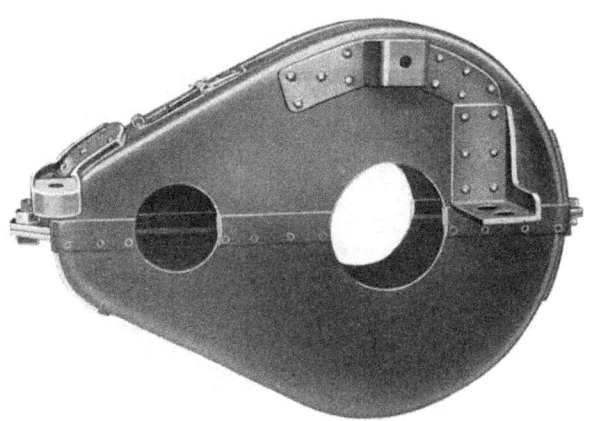

For General Electric 80-A Motor

Keystone Steel Gear Cases

Rightly named "The Cases of Service." They are made of the very best grade of soft, open-hearth, deep-drawing sheet steel that can be bought; sheets are both riveted and electrically spot-welded together; this, together with the grade of steel used, assumes a strong, tight, rigid gear case, and one that *stays* strong, tight and rigid.

Nose brackets are solid castings, riveted to the case through six thicknesses of metal. Side brackets are of hot pressed steel, securely riveted to the case through four thicknesses of metal. Keystone bracket supporting systems are typical of the strength and durability of the entire case.

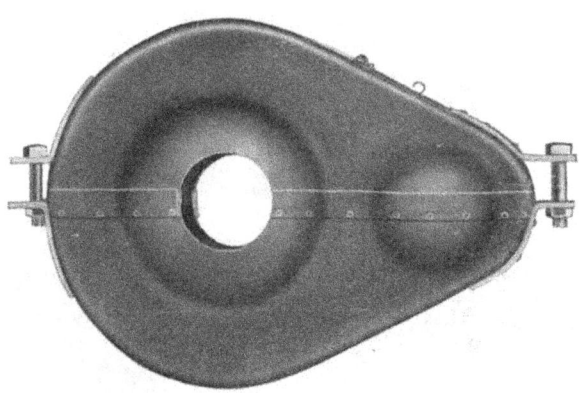

For General Electric 57 Motor

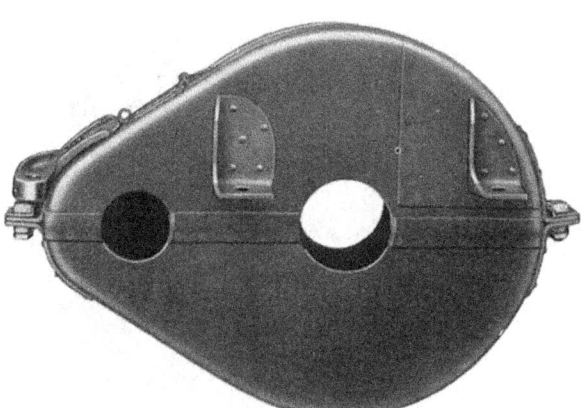

For Westinghouse 49 Motor

Keystone Steel Gear Cases

Keystone Steel Gear Cases are light in weight, easy to repair if damaged, easy to install and inspect, save money in cost of current required to haul around as compared with malleables.

Made for practically all modern types of railway motors and for a variety of mining and industrial motors. They can be furnished for motors other than those listed in our Supplement to Catalog No. 4, Vol. 2, upon receipt of complete specifications.

KEYSTONE QUALITY

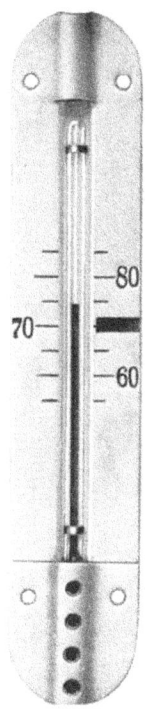

Keystone Car
Thermometer

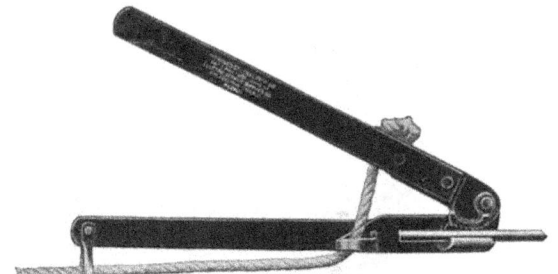

Improved St. Louis Trolley
Pick-up

Trolley Pick-up in Special
Glass Front Box

Fused Car Lighting
Switch

F P Car Replacer

KEYSTONE QUALITY

Motorman's Shade
Pay - Within Car Type

Wear-Proof Mat

THE CLASSIC 1911 TROLLEY CAR BUILDER'S REFERENCE BOOK

ELECTRIC RAILWAY DICTIONARY

By Rodney Hitt
Associate Editor, Electric Railway Journal

REPRINTED BY PERISCOPEFILM.COM

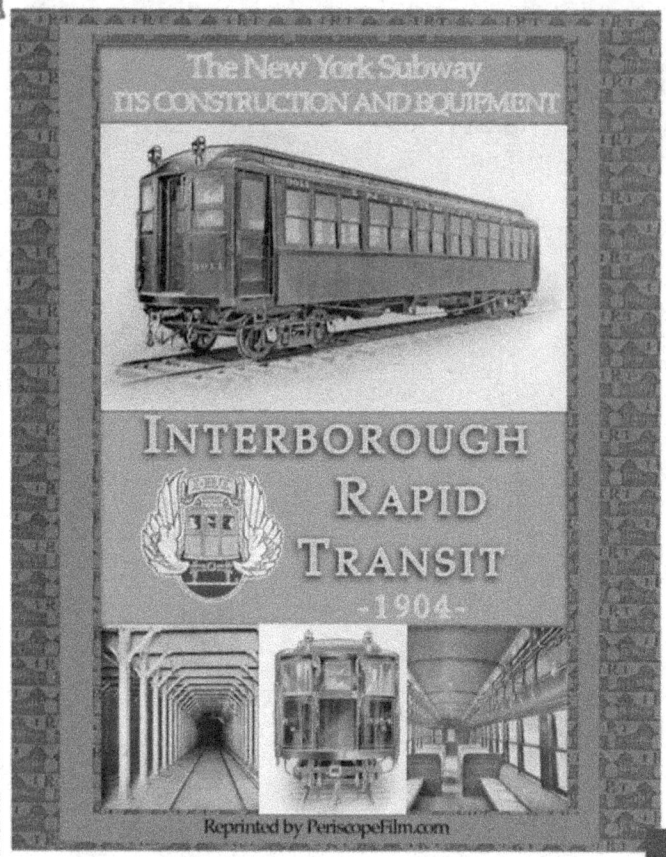

On October 27, 1904, the Interborough Rapid Transit Company opened the first subway in New York City. Running between City Hall and 145th Street at Broadway, the line was greeted with enthusiasm and, in some circles, trepidation. Created under the supervision of Chief Engineer S.L.F. Deyo, the arrival of the IRT foreshadowed the end of the "elevated" transit era on the island of Manhattan. The subway proved such a success that the IRT Co. soon achieved a monopoly on New York public transit. In 1940 the IRT and its rival the BMT were taken over by the City of New York. Today, the IRT subway lines still exist, primarily in Manhattan where they are operated as the "A Division" of the subway. Reprinted here is a special book created by the IRT, recounting the design and construction of the fledgling subway system. Originally created in 1904, it presents the IRT story with a flourish, and with numerous fascinating illustrations and rare photographs.

Originally written in the late 1900's and then periodically revised, A History of the Baldwin Locomotive Works chronicles the origins and growth of one of America's greatest industrial-era corporations. Founded in the early 1830's by Philadelphia jeweler Matthais Baldwin, the company built a huge number of steam locomotives before ceasing production in 1949. These included the 4-4-0 American type, 2-8-2 Mikado and 2-8-0 Consolidation. Hit hard by the loss of the steam engine market, Baldwin soldiered on for a brief while, producing electric and diesel engines. General Electric's dominance of the market proved too much, and Baldwin finally closed its doors in 1956. By that time over 70,500 Baldwin locomotives had been produced. This high quality reprint of the official company history dates from 1920. The book has been slightly reformatted, but care has been taken to preserve the integrity of the text.

NOW AVAILABLE AT
WWW.PERISCOPEFILM.COM

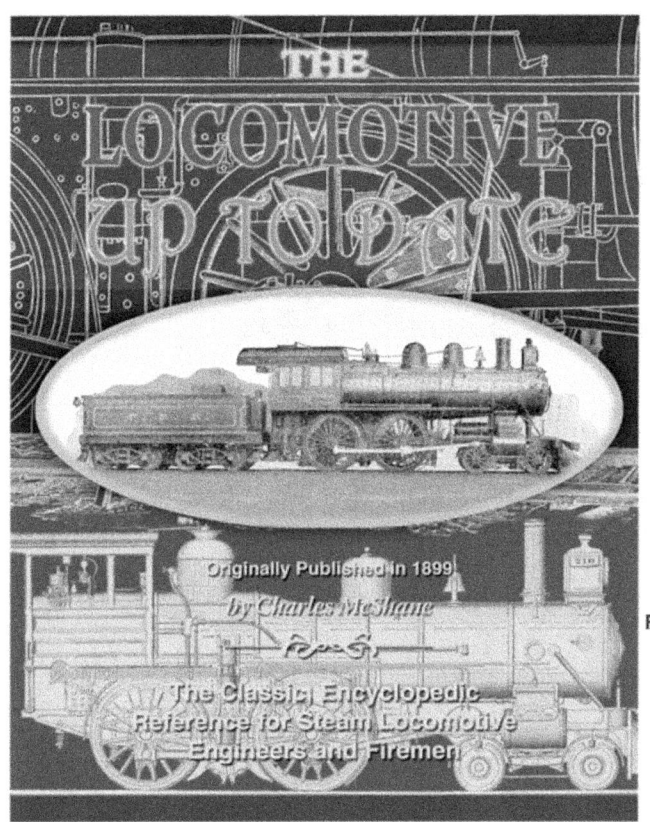

When it was originally published in 1899, **The Locomotive Up to Date** was hailed as "...the most definitive work ever published concerning the mechanism that has transformed the American nation: the steam locomotive." Filled with over 700 pages of text, diagrams and photos, this remains one of the most important railroading books ever written. From steam valves to sanders, trucks to side rods, it's a treasure trove of information, explaining in easy-to-understand language how the most sophisticated machines of the 19th Century were operated and maintained. This new edition is an exact duplicate of the original. Reformatted as an easy-to-read 8.5x11 volume, it's delightful for railroad enthusiasts of all ages.

Originally printed in 1898 and then periodically revised, **The Motorman...and His Duties** served as the definitive training text for a generation of streetcar operators. A must-have for the trolley or train enthusiast, it is also an important source of information for museum staff and docents. Lavishly illustrated with numerous photos and black and white line drawings, this affordable reprint contains all of the original text. Includes chapters on trolley car types and equipment, troubleshooting, brakes, controllers, electricity and principles, electric traction, multi-car control and has a convenient glossary in the back. If you've ever operated a trolley car, or just had an electric train set, this is a terrific book for your shelf!

ALSO NOW AVAILABLE FROM PERISCOPEFILM.COM!

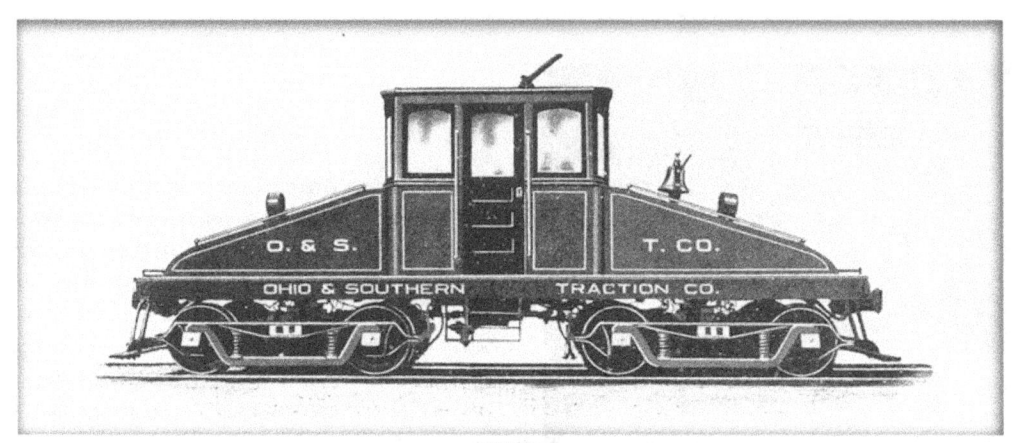

©2010 Periscope Film LLC
All Rights Reserved
ISBN #978-1-935700-33-3
www.PeriscopeFilm.com

www.ingramcontent.com/pod-product-compliance
Lightning Source LLC
LaVergne TN
LVHW061347060426
835512LV00012B/2592